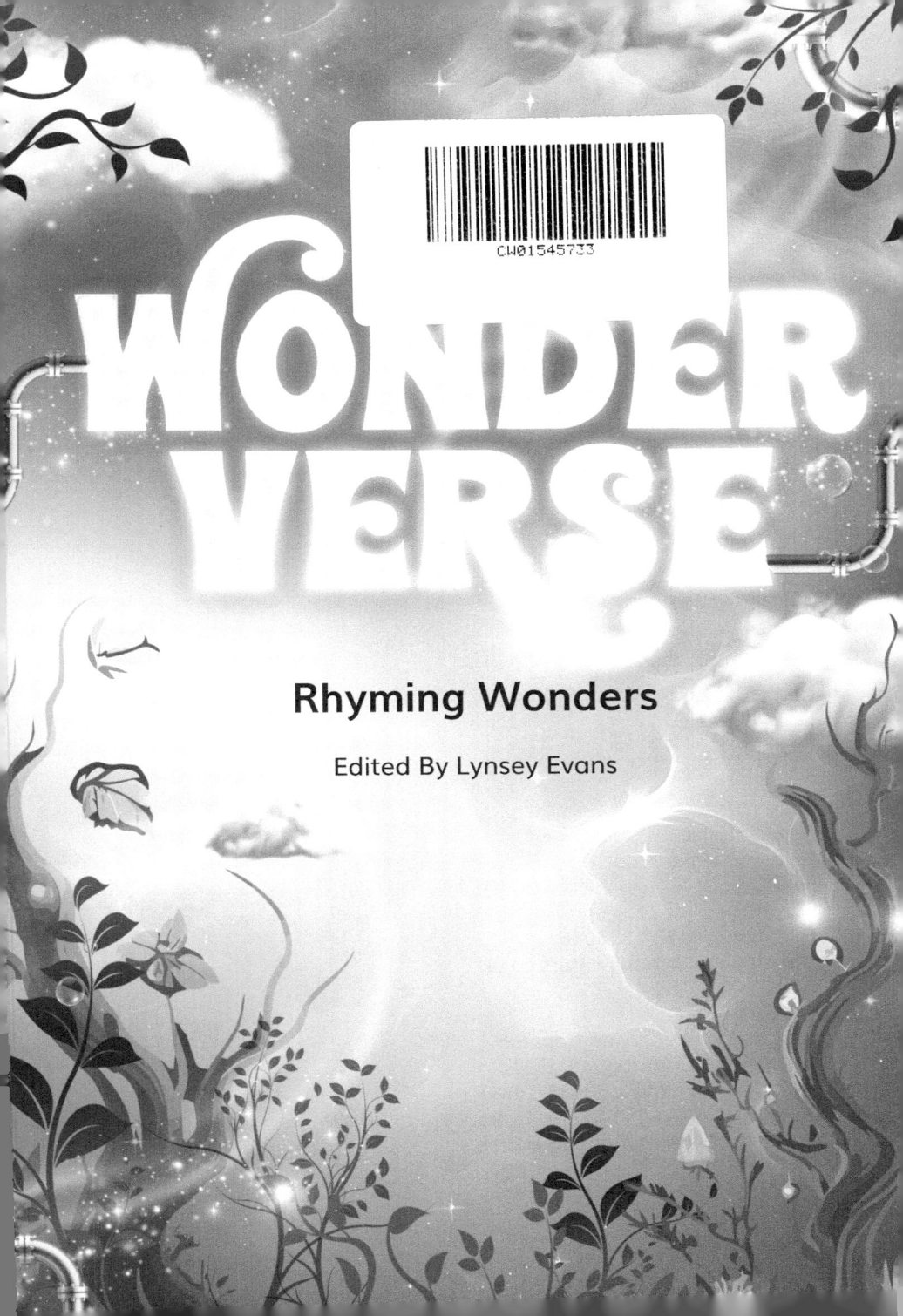

WONDER VERSE

Rhyming Wonders

Edited By Lynsey Evans

First published in Great Britain in 2025 by:

Young Writers
Remus House
Coltsfoot Drive
Peterborough
PE2 9BF
Telephone: 01733 890066
Website: www.youngwriters.co.uk

All Rights Reserved
Book Design by Davina Hopping
© Copyright Contributors 2024
Softback ISBN 978-1-83685-108-0
Printed and bound in the UK by BookPrintingUK
Website: www.bookprintinguk.com
YB0622Q

FOREWORD

WELCOME READER,

For Young Writers' latest competition *Wonderverse*, we asked primary school pupils to explore their creativity and write a poem on any topic that inspired them. They rose to the challenge magnificently with some going even further and writing stories too! The result is this fantastic collection of writing in a variety of styles.

Here at Young Writers our aim is to encourage creativity in children and to inspire a love of the written word, so it's great to get such an amazing response, with some absolutely fantastic pieces. This open theme of this competition allowed them to write freely about something they are interested in, which we know helps to engage kids and get them writing. Within these pages you'll find a variety of topics, from hopes, fears and dreams, to favourite things and worlds of imagination. The result is a collection of brilliant writing that showcases the creativity and writing ability of the next generation.

I'd like to congratulate all the young writers in this anthology, I hope this inspires them to continue with their creative writing.

CONTENTS

Hanford School, Child Okeford

Bea Mischi (10)	1
Emily Fox-Pitt (10)	2
Eliza Robinson (10)	3
Octavia Plunkett (9)	4
Henrietta Heppenstall (10)	5
Florrie Holland (10)	6
Jemima Sellick (10)	7
Sofia Pardo (10)	8
Beatrix Glendenning (9)	9
Allegra Aitken (9)	10
Grace Strauss (10)	11
Lola Gonzalez (10)	12
Bella Guinness (10)	13
Beatrice Francis (10)	14
Cordelia Plunkett (10)	15
Georgie Bagley (9)	16
Lucia Xie (9)	17
Amelia Leach (9)	18

Rice Lane Primary School, Liverpool

Lilah Fletcher (10)	19
Ava Fernandez (10)	20
Sofia Tyrrell (11)	22
Sophie Mason (10)	23
Malachy Patrick (10)	24
Lucy Edwards (9)	26
Olivia Toner (9)	27
Freya Gregory (9)	28
Allan Mavuto (9)	29
Isaac Spence (10)	30
Martha Taylor (10)	31
Cali Gray (10) & Lois Sheridan (9)	32

Sophie Cunliffe (9) & Emily McDermott (8)	33
Ellena Douglas (9)	34
Sophie MacDonald (10)	35
Maya Sutton Nielsen (10)	36
Lillie Macfarlane (9)	37
Jathursa Uthayakaran (10) & Phoebe	38
Chloe Horrocks (10)	39

Rushey Mead Primary School, Leicester

Nisarg Suman (10)	40
Kishan Patel (10)	42
Yug Mukesh (10)	43
Mayank Salanki (11)	44
Khashni Ramdas (10)	45
Chreshta Deva (10)	46
Mahi Carsane (11)	47
Aarav Kuikel (10)	48
Prusti Parikh (10)	49
Meghana Jivan (10)	50
Navya Gohel (10)	51

St Augustine Of Canterbury C of E VA Primary School, Belvedere

Temidayo Salako (10)	52
Zenzele Russell-Jess (10)	53
Ethan G (10)	54
Blessing Akeredolu (10)	55
Vivithra Arunagiri Babu Sailesh (10)	56
Tisa Prajapati (10)	57
Holly Ironside (10)	58

St Lewis Catholic Primary School, Croft

George Lander (9)	59
Miciah Thornton (9)	60
Emma Wall (9)	62
Thomas Warren (9)	64
Huw Barker (8)	65
Alice Mould (7)	66
Harper Barnes (7)	67
Ayrton Rushbrook (9)	68
Ruby Smith (9)	69
Aimen Jafar (9)	70
Tobias Mullin (10)	71
Hugo Wells (7)	72
Jan Herman (8)	73
Joseph Lander (7)	74
Annabelle (10)	75
Brenley Chadwick (9)	76
Alice Walker (8)	77
Stephanie Abe (8)	78
Louisa Howcroft (7)	79
Mary-Kate Wilkinson (11)	80
Samuel Whitehouse (8)	81
Harriet Smalley (10)	82
Sebastian Shaw (10)	83
Emily Morris (9)	84
Abigail Horton (9)	85
Elise Fogg (7)	86
Erin Quinn (10)	87
Phoebe Smith (8)	88
Andrew Alexander Bejcek Castillo (7)	89
India Seymour (11)	90
Zara Bishop (10)	91
Bella Morgan (10)	92
Artem Prokopenko (9)	93
Charley Seeby (10)	94
Jake Gould (8)	95
Libby Noonan (8)	96
Jack Baguley (8)	97
Tobias Chambers (9)	98
Blake Lyon (9)	99
Lincoln Starkey (7)	100
Frank William Bejcek Castillo (7)	101
Leo Rog (10)	102
Sophia Bishop (8)	103
Kaiden Patel (9)	104
Jacob Howkins (7)	105
Jacob Sherwin (9)	106
Kim Shaw (9)	107
Lachlan Waddell (8)	108
Evie Gallacher (8)	109

St Mark's C of E Primary School, Wigan

Darcie Minchin (8)	110
Amelia Ritchie (8)	111
Gracie Fenlon (8)	112
Lily Alice Morley (9)	113

St Mary's CE Primary School, Newchurch In Pendle

Olivia Norris (8)	114
Ollie Loach (8)	115
Amber Chambers-Storer (9)	116
William Treadwell (10)	117
Aurora Parkinson (9)	118
Freddie Standring (10)	119
Oliver Rimmer (8)	120
Oliver Marshall (7)	121
Max Birchenough (9)	122
Alexander Lyle (8)	123

The Russell School, Richmond

Gabriela Buchan (9)	124
Ani Sankisyan (9)	126
Adam Khadzhiev (9)	128
Jace Peacock (10)	129
Zachary Garcia-Sugarman (9)	130
Elodie M (9)	132
Niki Hezarkhani (9)	134
Camille Stanton (9)	135
Alex Sollier (9)	136
Kuzey Bahadir (9)	137

Kleo Svensson (10)	138
Frank Li (9)	139
Miray Jafarova (10)	140
Levi Versfeld (10)	141
Lukas Leung (9)	142
Luca Keyes (10)	143
Angelina Gofman (9)	144
Benjamin Reule (9)	145
Aurelia Logli (9)	146
Ellie (9)	147
Jason Ampavis (9)	148
Sofia Pallares (9)	149
Jude Bennett (9)	150
Teddy Mortlock (9)	151
Francis Shaw (9)	152
Cameron Lewin (9)	153
Nelly Noonan (9)	154
Scarlett Alboni (9)	155

The Russell School, Rickmansworth

Willow Papadopoulos (9)	156
Marceau Tysen Miles (9)	157
Evie Jakubowski (9)	158
Ruby Royan (9)	159
Millie Jakubowski (9)	160
Elizabeth Tredell (9)	161
Arabella Hooper (9)	162
Harry Toye (9)	163
Jessica Craft (10)	164
Everly Ball (9)	165
Ariana Parkinson (9)	166
Aalin Webber (9)	167
Evie Shah (9)	168

YOUNG WRITERS INFORMATION

We hope you have enjoyed reading this book – and that you will continue to in the coming years.

If you're the parent or family member of an enthusiastic poet or story writer, do visit our website **www.youngwriters.co.uk/subscribe** and sign up to receive news, competitions, writing challenges and tips, activities and much, much more! There's lots to keep budding writers motivated!

If you would like to order further copies of this book, or any of our other titles, then please give us a call or order via your online account.

Young Writers
Remus House
Coltsfoot Drive
Peterborough
PE2 9BF
(01733) 890066
info@youngwriters.co.uk

Join in the conversation!
Tips, news, giveaways and much more!

The Day I Scored

The day I scored was the day it poured,
And the crowd went wild whilst my mum at the top smiled.
My kit was sparkling like a star so bright,
The ball was travelling to me with the speed of light
And, in one swift motion, I scored.

Evie Shah (9)
The Russell School, Rickmansworth

Football Dreams

My dream one day is to be a footballer
I must be big and strong
I must be quick and brave
The ball at my feet
The buzz of the crowd
A powerful shot
An outstretched hand
The back of the net
The winning goal
My teammates embrace me
My dream has come true.

Aalin Webber (9)
The Russell School, Rickmansworth

Autumn Is Here

Red, orange, yellow, green,
I crunch through the leaves as I walk.
I feel the wind brush past,
I think this season will last.

Conkers fall from twisting trees,
The scenery is like a rainbow of colours around.
It's that time for coats and hats and gloves.

Autumn is here.

Ariana Parkinson (9)
The Russell School, Rickmansworth

One Foggy Day On Halloween

On my way to school I see the trees,
Beginning to capture the fog.
The fog begins to creep and crawl up the spooky hills,
Until it reaches the graveyard next to my school.
At lunchtime, all the children could think of was Halloween
On the way home, we waved at the dead people in the graveyard.
We got home and ran up the steps to get our costumes.
"*Get in the car!*" shouted Mum.

Everly Ball (9)
The Russell School, Rickmansworth

Beautiful Night

The stars were twinkling, the lake was glistening
As I was listening to the sound of owls hooting
The wolves were howling to the beautiful moon
Soon I'll have to go and leave this wonderful place
For it has nearly struck ten and my mum will be calling for me to come home
So, I say on my phone,
"Five more minutes."
I kept walking and walking till something made me jump
I fell on a rock and landed with a thump
Waking up in my own bed, was it a dream?
Why am I so keen?

Jessica Craft (10)
The Russell School, Rickmansworth

Cosmic

Ten... nine... eight... seven... six... five... four... three... two... one...
Blast-off!
Flying through the darkness of space.
Flying past planets that were never on the map.
The infinite darkness engulfed all types of light.
Soaring past wonderful and wacky-shaped asteroids.
In a dynamic movement, something flies past,
A UFO for a chance.
I think to myself,
No one will believe me,
I land,
I tell everyone.
As I thought,
No one ever did believe me.
So, it was my secret.

Harry Toye (9)
The Russell School, Rickmansworth

The Sea

As she sways about,
With her cold blue water,
There is no doubt,
That humans hate her,

Humans don't realise their crimes,
That they've done on her,
Maybe if we'd stop all the time,
That's what she would prefer.

Animals live under her,
The most beautiful in the world,
That's where fish lurk,
And also some pearls!

She is proud of what she is,
Because there are no other seas,
Although she does miss
Everyone swimming just after *tea!*

Arabella Hooper (9)
The Russell School, Rickmansworth

In A Jar

You can catch a Zinglezanglezork,
In a jar, in a jar, in a jar,
You can catch a Lalalololay,
In a jar, in a jar, in a jar.

But inspiration flies as free as a bird,
As a deer in the woods,
Like a song only heard,
By the ears of a baby crying to be heard.

You can catch a Rubbleribblerabble,
In a jar, in a jar, in a jar,
You can catch a Bibblybobblybabbly,
In a jar, in a jar, in a jar.

So, I hope you find your inspiration.
It will not be in a jar.
But I'm sure it won't be far!

Elizabeth Tredell (9)
The Russell School, Rickmansworth

Winter In November

As the snow falls,
When you're walking in the woods.
It's getting pretty cold,
You must put up your hood.

Wrap yourself up,
Make sure you are warm.
Hurry! Get inside,
As there might be a storm...

Is it winter in November?
No one seems to know,
Who doesn't like this weather?
Don't we all like snow?

The trees become all fluffy,
As the robins sing their songs.
I think it's winter in November,
Am I right or wrong?

You can stay inside your house,
Or go outside in the cold.
I know I like the snow,
Do you?

Millie Jakubowski (9)
The Russell School, Rickmansworth

The Odd Farm

Once, there was a farm,
A farmer and a barn
Some strange animals in it,
That not many people would visit
Why?
There was an ostrich with a tremendous beak,
A bulldog which was 'quite a freak'
A crazy monkey, a hairy baboon
A pufferfish that blew up like a balloon.
Not very normal, as you can see,
There was also a ferocious tiger
That was scared of bees.
A stripeless zebra, a rainbow cat,
A silly sheep that loved to chat.
So, if you come upon this farm,
Don't be scared, they mean no harm.
They are all perfect in their own way,
They make our world complete each day.

Ruby Royan (9)
The Russell School, Rickmansworth

In The Woods

The trees swayed in the whispering winds,
And something was heard above,
It turned out it was just a bird singing,
And it looked like it was a dove.

The fox was heard from many miles away,
Just scattering around for food.
But when he heard the tree sway,
That didn't do him any good.

A deer was spotted in the grass,
Looking around at the sunset
Until he met the little orange fox,
This was something he could never forget.

All these animals in the woods,
Jumping and flying with joy.
They would always be happy,
Always and forever!
This is something we could never annoy!

Evie Jakubowski (9)
The Russell School, Rickmansworth

In The Forest

The trees whispered secrets as the faint breeze blew,
In the sunset's gaze, the trees looked like shadows, vast and black,
The chirps of the evening birds lifted hope,
But still the thought of night haunted them like a nightmare.

As the last sliver of sun disappeared,
A cold darkness swept across the woods.
Somewhere from the deep forest,
A wolf howled with anger and despair.

The full moon appeared as white as chalk,
Bigger than ever before.
All the animals stopped in their tracks,
To gaze at the beautiful sight.

Then, the morning bird called,
Joy had been found
And the sun began to reappear.

Marceau Tysen Miles (9)
The Russell School, Rickmansworth

How To Feel Great

Once, there was a girl called Willow,
In the mornings, she wouldn't leave her pillow.
When she woke up, she gave a ginormous yawn,
Why did she feel like this every single morn?

She was too sleepy to play with her friends,
So, she spent break time doing some bends
But, by lunchtime, she was so sleepy again.

Her friends wouldn't play with her so sad and alone,
Oh she tried, oh she tried not to crumble and moan.
By dinnertime, her eyelids were drooping and sore,
She could almost fall asleep on the hard wooden floor.

Aching and heavy, she crawled up the stairs,
Then, she collapsed in a heap on her teddy bears.

"Oh, this is too much," she said,
"I must get myself earlier to bed"
She thought of her bad ways, she needed to change.
"Early nights must be the key!" she exclaimed.

Willow Papadopoulos (9)
The Russell School, Rickmansworth

The Elephants

Two wrinkled eyes
One tiny tail
Two flapping ears

Marching, stamping, thrashing
Grey and wise
Like an enormous brick wall
Wisest of them all!

Scarlett Alboni (9)
The Russell School, Richmond

What Food Is Your Type?

What type of food is your favourite to eat?
Do you like vegetables?
Do you like meat?
Do you like apples?
Do you like pears?
Do you like kiwis wrapped in hairs?

Nelly Noonan (9)
The Russell School, Richmond

Nature

On the dark lime grass,
Green blunt blades of spring,
A carpet for feet.

When the night starts
And birds go to hide in nests,
They will rest for strength.

Cameron Lewin (9)
The Russell School, Richmond

My Hungry Dog

Every open fridge,
Every sandwich made,
Every bite of steak,
I am wide awake watching you!

Every single day,
Every single night,
Every single dream,
The bacon summons me...

Francis Shaw (9)
The Russell School, Richmond

Poppies

We wear the poppies for the World War
For all the people who lost their lives in the World War
The soldiers who sacrificed their lives for us
We have poppies because they are the flowers that grew in the fields.

Teddy Mortlock (9)
The Russell School, Richmond

Remembrance

I am super thankful for the men who fought for our freedom
Being brave like tigers

We remember the young people who joined early to save us
Every year on the 11th of November, at the 11th hour on the 11th day.

Jude Bennett (9)
The Russell School, Richmond

Wednesday

She creeps up to you
And her scary little hand helps her
And goes on adventures
She plays her cello really beautifully
She's made an awful friend
And when the awful friend touches water
Snake scales come on her arm.

Sofia Pallares (9)
The Russell School, Richmond

Rain

Rain
Such a
Dreadful pain
No one wants it
In sight, it's so lame
Doesn't even give you any light.
As blue as sadness, people think it's
Madness! But without rain, all the
Poor plants would
Complain!
And it would be a shame...

Jason Ampavis (9)
The Russell School, Richmond

The Cat On The Mat

There once was a cat who sat on a mat
He took a nap until he heard *snap!*
It was a man in a hat
Saying, "That's not a mat, it's my map!"
Cats jump as high as the Eiffel Tower
His nose is as wet as a pool of Welsh water
Cats are fluffy like a ball of rabbit's fur
The cat's fur is as black as a solar eclipse.

Ellie (9)
The Russell School, Richmond

Chores Time

H ow do you get your mum off your back when it's chores o'clock?
E xclaim you're ill and draw on chickenpox.
L isten to me if you weep and weep.
P ossibly because you have energy, she will make you sweep

M aybe you don't agree, but it will set you free.
E xample - then you have TV and you can just be.

Aurelia Logli (9)
The Russell School, Richmond

Dinosaurs

Pterodactyl has some cool features
And it's spelt with a silent 'P'
It is pretty free
Roaming the sky of Sicily

Stegosaurus has some spikes
To fend off predators
Blood goes in the plates, yikes

Velociraptor is fast and furious
And also very curious

Spinosaurus' teeth are sharp
To chomp through fish and carp.

Benjamin Reule (9)
The Russell School, Richmond

What Am I?

I am green,
I am always seen,
In autumn I fall down,
Then I turn yellow, orange or brown,
What am I?

I live up high,
Technically in the sky,
The wind blows me around,
Which makes a whistling sound,
What am I?

There are different types of me,
Caterpillars like to eat me too,
I have a nice view,
Of everything, everyone and you,
What am I?

Answer: Leaves.

Angelina Gofman (9)
The Russell School, Richmond

Minecraft

Houses are destroyed
Villages are quite small
Boom! Crash! TNT explodes
Chunks of earth are scattered around the environment

When the sky turns black

The terrifying zombies and creepers come out
A fire alights, and they disappear into the abyss

Armour made out of steel and iron
Rusty and tough
Protects from slashes
Steve fights back.

Luca Keyes (10)
The Russell School, Richmond

I Don't Like...

I don't like metaphors,
They make my heart feel like stone.

I don't like similes,
They make my legs feel as rubbery as an eraser.

I don't like personification,
It makes my eyeballs dance in my eyes.

I don't like alliteration,
It makes my arms feel like wobbly walruses.

I don't like repetition,
I don't like repetition,
I don't like repetition.

Lukas Leung (9)
The Russell School, Richmond

Coco

I'm a meat eater,
I waggle my tail,
I do the cha-cha when I see my momma,
I do the zoom-zoom when I see my papa,
I steal socks and take them outside for the fox to have,
I jump and steal food,
I hate vegetables,
I run like The Flash,
My ears flop when I run,
I'm a grasshopper because I jump in the grass,
I play hide 'n' seek,
Don't you know who I am yet?

Answer: Coco, the working cocker spaniel.

Levi Versfeld (10)
The Russell School, Richmond

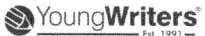

Mine And Your Favourite Season

The leaves are starting to get rusty
You start to wear your coat
Even mittens and hats
What season am I?!

Throw away your coats
And bring out your shorts
Eat as many ice creams as you want
What season am I?!

Brrr! It's really cold
Go out and make snowmen
Drink hot chocolate all day
What season am I?!

Here come the fabulous flowers
And here comes the sun (yay!)
Maybe take off a few layers of clothes
What season am I?!

Miray Jafarova (10)
The Russell School, Richmond

The Wonders Of Summer

Leaves green, trees tall,
Seeds have a little chat in the underground hall,
Flowers colourful and dandelions fluffy,
Ponds blue and nettles spiky.

Apples red, pears ripe,
Blackberries black, strawberries reddish pink,
Lemons yellowed and mangoes green,
Grapes purple and tomatoes orangey-lime.

Trees stretch to the bright blue sky,
As worms plough the soil to help them grow,
The bark is rough and brown,
Trees play a special role in cleaning the air,
And give us shade.

Frank Li (9)
The Russell School, Richmond

The Little Boat's Journey At Sea

It giggles and wiggles on its journey at sea
With its little orange flag
The ocean pushes it backwards and forwards
Like a lever on its journey
The waves crash against rocks
Slapping the sand with its large hands
The little red boat awaits its destination
On its journey at sea

Little fishes
Swim and prance
Laughing and giggling
In their secret hiding space,
Away from the sharks and
The predators and people
They swim around
And make you laugh and that's
A fish.

Kleo Svensson (10)
The Russell School, Richmond

The Orca's Story

K iller whale: largest ocean dolphin
I nteresting, but as lethal as a weapon
L oves to eat fish, sharks, rays and seals
L ives in the deep ocean waters like a king
E ats with rows of sharp, jagged teeth
R ips apart dolphins and whales easily

W hat a killing machine he is
H e grows to eighteen feet in length
A nd fish are scared of him
L arge boats struggle to pull orcas out of the water
E very ocean animal respects his majestic reign.

Kuzey Bahadir (9)
The Russell School, Richmond

Jamie Smart?!

Jamie Smart, he is a fart!
He writes books and they are the best,
They should be in a fun fest!
They're Looshkin!
One minute he is in bed,
The next, the world is falling apart!
Plus he's got a companion called Bear!
That is a teddy bear!
The song about him goes like this:

He's Bear
He's Bear
He's made of human hair!
He's Bear
He's Bear
He's made of human hair!
Touch his nose and his head grows!

Jamie Smart, he is a fart!
He has written more but we have run out of space!
Boom!

Alex Sollier (9)
The Russell School, Richmond

Who Am I?

Once a year at 8 at night
Just before Christmas when the old man strikes
Just after summer it takes all bright and turns it into fright

Carve out your pumpkins
Be ready for goblins
Bats and cats run down streets
On cobweb sheets
Prepare to say trick or treat?

Cool cats, zany zombies and witchy witches
Beautiful costumes made with stitches
Ghostly ghouls, vicious vampires and menacing mummies
All trying to fill their tummies

Chocolate, sweets, lollipops and candy
Cotton candy festivals filled with laughter
Knock, knock on your door
Who am I?

Halloween!

Camille Stanton (9)
The Russell School, Richmond

I Am Death

I creep up on you while you rest,
I'll serve you what you deserve,
My name shall reign, I am the best,
I swoop and glide, I turn and swerve.

Some call me a danger, others a pest,
That rings in my head like a tiny bell,
My name shall reign, I am the best,
Underestimate me and I'll send you to Hell.

Destroying lives is my quest,
Because I'm evil to the bone,
My name shall reign, I am the best,
So, naturally, I have a heart of stone.

The black death was the gold in the chest,
Wars and battles are so much fun,
My name shall reign, I am the best,
I am the moon, not the sun.

Niki Hezarkhani (9)
The Russell School, Richmond

A wesome autumn
U nbelievable beautiful colours
T urning into monsters
U nimaginable amount of sweets
M esmerising pumpkins
N oisy explosions of fireworks.

Elodie M (9)
The Russell School, Richmond

Four Seasons

W ondrous magical Christmas
I nviting Jack Frost in
N ew toys
T orrential snowstorms
E veryone is cold
R eliable Santa

S plendid eggy Easter
P ollinating plants
R aging rain
I nteresting animals
N uts being found
G rand blooming flowers

S unny summer holidays
U pbeat hot sunshine
M arvellous memories
M agnificent colours in the garden
E ntertaining beach parties
R aucous barbecues

The Black Death is on its way,
Time to live your last day!

Zachary Garcia-Sugarman (9)
The Russell School, Richmond

The Black Death

He lurks through day and night,
They never know when he might strike.

He walks around through the city,
Showing no one any pity.

When he's your friend,
It's the end.

When they have a cough, they laugh it off,
But unknown to them, it's soon their end.

As the blisters swell,
They feel more unwell.

Black spores spread around the body,
Little do they know it's going to get bloody.

Pain and agony, whatever you say,
Soon it's going to be doomsday.

Vomiting and diarrhoea,
They'll never disappear,
As death is near.

Collected from their body is their soul,
Killing them and putting them in a hole.

The Xbox Chronicles

I'm slurping on this fish like a slush - no puppy
Only big dogs on my team, no guppies
I'm all around the map, can't track me
360 no scope if you attack me
Time is up, I'm on the way to the vault
If you get in my way, you'll get peppered, no salt
That's seasoning, you could call me a professional
Having dinner every night with hella vegetables
I cha-cha slide into your base
While I criss-cross glide all over the place
The name's J.A.C.E
Another Battle Royale won by me
This is Fortnite, it's time to sleep tight
So you'd better snooze, it's red vs blue
I'm never here to lose!

Jace Peacock (10)
The Russell School, Richmond

Death

In the heart of England, death came to call
A chilling silence hung over all
The black cloak of darkness spread far and wide
As he swept through the countryside

No soul was safe from his icy touch
As he claimed each life with a deadly clutch
From the bustling cities to the quiet leaves
Death's grip brought only sorrow and pain

The once merry faces now pale with fear
As the end drew near, death's whisper clear
No one could escape his relentless grasp
As he moved with a speed so vast

Villages emptied, towers lay still
As death's shadow crept over every hill
No sound but the wailing of the wind
As England's fate was cruelly pinned
The rivers ran red with the blood of the slain
As death's presence brought only disdain, no hope of salvation
No chance of reprieve
As the land was consumed by grief.

Adam Khadzhiev (9)
The Russell School, Richmond

Not too hot or not too cold, it's just the right amount,
It feels like summer or maybe autumn
But it isn't either,
All you have to know is that you need
A woolly coat because it rains all day,
What season am I?
Spring!

Ani Sankisyan (9)
The Russell School, Richmond

The Seasons Of The Year!

All of the fallen leaves that I crunch through
Go red, orange and gold
The smell of the bonfires in the distance
Smell like a dragon's own breath that curls up in the sky
What season am I?
Autumn!

All of the beaches look so warm
That the breeze floats away into the distance
It feels so short but if you think about it
It's actually been 60 days or so
What season am I?
Summer!

It's the time of year where it gets so cold
You need a woolly hat
But all you want to say is *no!*
You build a snowman in the snow
Or snow angels on the floor
What season am I?
Winter!

Happiness is a boppy bunny,
It jumps all around you.
Its yellow hand jumps out
And tickles your tummy.
It makes you want to laugh,
It makes you want to sing,
Bing, bing, bing.

Calmness is the last one,
A green little blob.
You do not sob,
It makes you feel keen to be seen,
Smiling and laughing,
Forever and ever.

Gabriela Buchan (9)
The Russell School, Richmond

Emotion

Anger is a red ball of fire,
As bad as can be,
It puts a scary shadow over you,
So you cannot see.
It makes you want to frown,
It makes you scream.
After all that, it makes you feel down.

Sadness is a blue blob,
Which sits, lonely, on the floor,
It creeps along the corridor,
Making no sound at all.
It makes you want to cry,
Sometimes, you feel like you want to sigh.
It is not a nice feeling,
But it's good at dealing with.

Fear is a gloomy, grey old thing,
Which is the opposite to singing.
It makes you want to shiver
And it makes you want to shake.
You might sweat
At this threat.

Mr Penguin

P eople have jobs.
E at food to live.
N ext is a shop.
G iraffes are the tallest animal.
U ncle is bald.
I like pineapple.
N elson Mandela changed the world.

Alexander Lyle (8)
St Mary's CE Primary School, Newchurch In Pendle

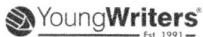

My Friends Are My Best Friends

I've been lucky to find
My best friends
They are so kind
My best friends
We love to laugh
My best friends
When we run down the path
My best friends
Even when we're quiet as mice
My best friends
Are twice as nice
My best friends.

Max Birchenough (9)
St Mary's CE Primary School, Newchurch In Pendle

Beautiful Dogs Around The World

Dogs can be so intelligent but we don't know why.
They can be trained, big or small,
all you have to do is try.
They can be trained to do tricks and sit for a treat.
They can bark very loud and be so sweet.
They can have long or short hair.
They wag their tail and really care.

Beautiful dogs around the world!

Oliver Marshall (7)
St Mary's CE Primary School, Newchurch In Pendle

Pokémon

P idgeot soars through the bright blue sky,
O shawott surfs on the walloping waves,
K angaskhan lurks in the deep dark caves,
É evee has eight exciting evolutions,
M eowth is a feline, most mischievous,
O ddish will send you straight to sleep,
N idoran's horn poisons its prey.

Oliver Rimmer (8)
St Mary's CE Primary School, Newchurch In Pendle

Space

Look up at the millions of stars
In the little tiny gaps, you might be able to see a big red planet called Mars
Far, far away, we have Saturn with its rings
Some may say it looks like it has wings
Pluto may be small, but I'm sure it's bigger than a ball
But, among all these planets, there is the Milky Way that moves at a pace.

Freddie Standring (10)
St Mary's CE Primary School, Newchurch In Pendle

Animals

Animals are amazing,
like rabbits that like racing.
Or the dogs that are in the pound,
and the meerkats that go up and down.
Also, there's the crocodile with its big jaws,
or the bears with their humongous paws.
And the bumblebee that you see,
also, there's the tiger who came to tea.
Fairies are fantastic,
and worms that are not elastic.

Animals are amazing.

Aurora Parkinson (9)
St Mary's CE Primary School, Newchurch In Pendle

Biking

I love biking
I started when I was two
It's the funniest thing ever
Even when I am blue
I always jump up even after a tear or two
Keep on going even if I overdo
New bike every once in a while
I never stand like a statue
Always peddling like a race car in disguise
Forever energised looking carefully with my eyes
If I stop I will realise how happy biking makes my life.

William Treadwell (10)
St Mary's CE Primary School, Newchurch In Pendle

Friendship

Friendship, friendship, nothing like it.
The world has lots of opportunities to make friends.
True friends always help you when you need it.
Friends stick together forever.
True friends accept your ideas.
When you have friends, life is easy.
When you don't have friends, life gets harder and harder.
Seeing all the kids playing with friends.
Friends, friends, friends are so important in life.
God made us like this so we can be different and make our own choices and own friends.
Friends are great, lovely, calming and beautiful.

Amber Chambers-Storer (9)
St Mary's CE Primary School, Newchurch In Pendle

Emotions

Happiness is like the sun shining on your back when you're sad,
Sadness is like rain that does not want to go away, a negative feeling,
Shock feels like a danger that jumps out from behind your back,
Boredom feels like something that will not go away and demolishes your creativity,
Anger is like something that takes over your body in rage,
Disgust feels like gross slugs climbing on your face,
Surprise feels like a cute, warm, cuddly jumper out of the wardrobe,
Fear is like when a wasp goes to sting you,
Love feels like when you find the person you are meant to be with,
Grief is like when something you love dies,
Envy feels like when you see something that you really want but you can't have it,
Humour feels like everything is right in the world.

Ollie Loach (8)
St Mary's CE Primary School, Newchurch In Pendle

My Year

January brings the snow,
Get my sledge and off I go,
February is cold and icy,
Feed me something hot and spicy,
March is here and strong winds blow,
Wrap up warm from head to toe,
April comes and it won't stop raining,
Can't play golf says Dad complaining,
May and now it's birthday time,
A lovely puppy and he's mine,
June at last the sun is shining,
Let's ride my horse and go rock climbing,
July then August, holidays are coming,
Pack my case and see me running,
September back to school too soon,
Learn about space and the moon,
October, November with Christmas around the corner,
I don't want a pie like Little Jack Horner,
December let's decorate the tree,
That's all for now and it's goodbye from me.

Olivia Norris (8)
St Mary's CE Primary School, Newchurch In Pendle

Little Mrs Viky And Her Friend

Little Mrs Viky went out one day
To fetch a pail of water.
She went back home and had a bath
Then went to the park to meet her friend
And play on the swings
And then went to Home Bargains.

Lily Alice Morley (9)
St Mark's C of E Primary School, Wigan

I Think You're Beautiful

Sometimes when skies are grey
A bird can fly past and make your day
When you're feeling pink
A worm might be on your left and give you a wink
Sometimes when you are blue
An animal may think of you
Some things may be fluffy
Some things may not
But either way, I think you're beautiful.

Gracie Fenlon (8)
St Mark's C of E Primary School, Wigan

Growing Up

Growing up growing up
Bigger and bigger
Every day until we
Stop!
Stop!
And stop!
We have to stop one day
Unless you want to be a giant!
Growing up would feel sad sometimes
Or happy or even excited
So if my legs, arms and feet (stinky)
Stop growing
I will become taller
Stronger
And a master!

Amelia Ritchie (8)
St Mark's C of E Primary School, Wigan

Our Solar System

First, there's the sun,
It's Earth's only one.
Next, there is Mercury,
There must be more, surely.
Next to Earth, you have Venus,
There's not a planet between us.
Earth follows on and some say it's flat,
It's round, not perfectly, but Mars is after that.
Jupiter is next, and then follows on Saturn,
Compared to the rest, it spins much faster.
Uranus is cold, it has thirteen rings,
Neptune has moons that make up sixteen.
Our solar system is vast, but it's a drop in the ocean,
46 billion light years each way, in the universe, we are woven.

Darcie Minchin (8)
St Mark's C of E Primary School, Wigan

What Am I?

What am I?
I have a long neck
I eat leaves high up from the trees
I am seen in zoos and jungles
What am I?

Answer: A giraffe.

Evie Gallacher (8)
St Lewis Catholic Primary School, Croft

My Idol

I am a footballer,
I play in blue and white,
Midfield is my position,
I'm originally from Scotland,
I used to play for Albion Rovers.

Who am I?

Lachlan Waddell (8)
St Lewis Catholic Primary School, Croft

The Little Girl In The Woods

F alling leaves,
O ut on the field,
R oses are red,
E very leaf falling from the tree,
S ky is blue,
T rees are green and brown.

Kim Shaw (9)
St Lewis Catholic Primary School, Croft

Rashford

R eady to tackle
A s fast as light
S teady
H umbling
F orward
O n the ball
R ed Devils
D angerous attacker.

Jacob Sherwin (9)
St Lewis Catholic Primary School, Croft

Riddle

Squishy, like a sun when rain comes
Wonderful, like a bright sun
I am round like a circle
I am colourful like a yellow rainbow
The inside of me is brighter than the outside of me.

Jacob Howkins (7)
St Lewis Catholic Primary School, Croft

The Red

The crowd,
Looking at the ref,
Everyone thinking
He is deaf.
When he blew the whistle,
The red shocked
Like a missile,
The manager's best,
Joined the rest.

Kaiden Patel (9)
St Lewis Catholic Primary School, Croft

Sports

S ports Day is an exciting event
P eople cheering for their team to win
O ther people competing for a trophy
R ugby is a sport like football
T esting new skills every day!

Sophia Bishop (8)
St Lewis Catholic Primary School, Croft

Gorillas

G orillas are nice,
O nly if you are nice,
R un, jump and parkour,
I ntelligent too,
L ove bananas,
L oving too,
A nd I love gorillas, don't you?

Leo Rog (10)
St Lewis Catholic Primary School, Croft

All About Hockey

H appy putting in the net,
O nly me in the room,
C heering on for my team, Manchester Storm,
K it of Manchester Storm is awesome,
E veryone smiling,
Y ou must go!

Frank William Bejcek Castillo (7)
St Lewis Catholic Primary School, Croft

What Am I?

I am big and furry,
I have big silver claws that can take animals' claws and paws,
I can take down people, so I eat meat,
You can find me in the wild.

What am I?

Answer: A bear.

Lincoln Starkey (7)
St Lewis Catholic Primary School, Croft

What Am I?

I am £1.99 in stores
I've got 10% coconut water, and vitamin B and E
I've got lots of flavours
I am a drink
Some are limited edition, rare
Some bottles glow in the dark

What am I?

Blake Lyon (9)
St Lewis Catholic Primary School, Croft

Christmas

C old air
H olidays
R eindeer
I love getting presents
S kiing down mountains
T rees with no leaves
M ovie night
A n early dusk
S nowy days.

Tobias Chambers (9)
St Lewis Catholic Primary School, Croft

When The Trees Get Cut Down

When the trees get cut down,
The animals have no home,
And the logs get chopped up in pieces,
And get wrapped up in something that looks like laces,
The animals have nowhere to live,
But they still won't give.

Jack Baguley (8)
St Lewis Catholic Primary School, Croft

The Fun But Spooky Riddle

What am I?
When I come around,
There is not a single sound,
So many sweets!
On this day, children get many treats,
In my bag, I have so much chocolate,
I have one big lolly,
I feel very jolly.
I am Halloween.

Libby Noonan (8)
St Lewis Catholic Primary School, Croft

Nightmare

N ight of terror
I am scared
G ame of terror
H aunted houses
T iny tippy toes
M ysterious paintings
A nnoying sounds
R ed blood disappearing
E nd goes me.

Jake Gould (8)
St Lewis Catholic Primary School, Croft

The Flame

Dragon flames burn down trees
Wood falls to the ground with a bang
Swirling through the air
His red scaly skin as hard as a rock
His beaming eyes staring at you
He hisses like a steam engine
While swooping his tail angrily.

Charley Seeby (10)
St Lewis Catholic Primary School, Croft

Autumn

A utumn is my favourite time of year
U nder our feet, animals sleep
T he leaves gold, red and orange
U p and away, birds fly
M y favourite day is my birthday
N o one wants to sleep on Halloween.

Artem Prokopenko (9)
St Lewis Catholic Primary School, Croft

Summertime Fun

S ummer is the best time of year
U nder the sun in the swimming pool
M emories lasting for a lifetime
M osquitoes flying all around
E ating ice cream every day
R emember the splashes and fun that we had.

Bella Morgan (10)
St Lewis Catholic Primary School, Croft

Magical Unicorn

It is as big as a dog
And as beautiful as a rainbow
It is as gentle as a cute bunny
It's an amazing animal
It is amazing like sweets
It has got a lovely magical horn
Do not make it angry or it will go grey
It's a unicorn.

Zara Bishop (10)
St Lewis Catholic Primary School, Croft

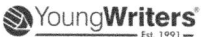

The Lurking Monster

M onster lurking in the break,
O n the way to eat you!
N o one has seen him, know him,
S trong as titanium,
T earing everything in front of him.
E xpected when least expected,
R eady to follow you.

India Seymour (11)
St Lewis Catholic Primary School, Croft

Football

Football is as...

F un as scoring,
O ffside goals are not given,
O pen space, everywhere,
T ouching into the space,
B est in goal,
A lways passing,
L ove to celebrate,
L ove to save goals.

Andrew Alexander Bejcek Castillo (7)
St Lewis Catholic Primary School, Croft

Look Out For Ladybugs

L ots of bugs at school
A nts, spiders and butterflies
D on't kill them all
Y ou should take care not to step on them
B e careful! Don't touch a spiderweb
U nder shoes, if you step on them
G reat to look at.

Phoebe Smith (8)
St Lewis Catholic Primary School, Croft

The Floating Bike

The floating bike rides around
Faster than light
All you can hear is a ringing bell
No one can tell
Who hides
Around at dark
The hooded biker
Their name unknown
Who will make this poem known?
Only you
Tell me it's true
It's you.

Erin Quinn (10)
St Lewis Catholic Primary School, Croft

Koala

K nowing cute animals so fluffy and grey,
O n top of a brown branch, people drink tea whilst watching them,
A ustralia is full of them,
L owering down my favourite tree is mean, crash, down it goes!
A t the zoo now all safe and clean, what shall I do?

Elise Fogg (7)
St Lewis Catholic Primary School, Croft

Blank Room But There's No Escape

"It's spooky season," shouted Dior excitedly
Time to make a ghost, *aargh!*
"Wait, where am I? *Aargh!*" shouted Dior.
The darkness stole the light from the room
There was a candle as she ran out
As she reached out to the candle, it disappeared.

Abigail Horton (9)
St Lewis Catholic Primary School, Croft

Christmas Is Here

I am that time of year that brings a cup of cheer
Lots of people looking at me I am as merry as can be
I am in December and everybody loves me
Puddings, mmm... delicious
Little people with pointy hats flying around
No, stop! presents everywhere
What am I?

I am Christmas!

Emily Morris (9)
St Lewis Catholic Primary School, Croft

What Am I?

I'm a football team.
I wear the colour red.
I play in the Premier League.
My nickname is the Red Devils.
Our sponsor is Snapdragon.
The stadium is the one and only Old Trafford.
Our rivals are Manchester City and Liverpool.
We have won fifty-four trophies.

What am I?

Sebastian Shaw (10)
St Lewis Catholic Primary School, Croft

My Amazing School

S tudents are the best
T eachers are the best.

L ove is our school,
E ncouragement is our school goal.
W e aim to make this school the best we can.
I n my years at St Lewis, it has been the best years.
S t Lewis is the best and it always will be.

Harriet Smalley (10)
St Lewis Catholic Primary School, Croft

Robo Dog

Robo dog is here
Everybody cheer
Woohoo, woohoo
Make sure he doesn't scratch you
Because he nearly got the flu
If he escapes, what will you do?
You might have to go to the loo.

He used to be a hero
But now he's zero
This is the end, make sure the dog doesn't hear.

Samuel Whitehouse (8)
St Lewis Catholic Primary School, Croft

St Lewis

S t Lewis is a wonderful place for the children,
T he teachers are amazing.

L earning in St Lewis is incredible,
E veryone is welcome in our school,
W e treat everyone with humanity and respect,
I love learning at St Lewis,
S t Lewis is a place for no bullies.

Mary-Kate Wilkinson (11)
St Lewis Catholic Primary School, Croft

Little Hedgehog

A s lovely as a hedgehog house.
U nbelievable as a big house for a small hedgehog.
T errific as a clear twinkly night under a hedgehog house in autumn
U nbeatable as a sweet hedgehog going into hibernation
M agic on Bonfire
N ight with a big loud bang, very scary for the little hedgehog.

Louisa Howcroft (7)
St Lewis Catholic Primary School, Croft

Swimming

Swimming is as...

S plashy as jumping in puddles
W et as rain
I n and out people go
M any hairs in the deep deep pool
M usty brown tiles, as brown as a leaf in autumn
I t's too easy for me
N ice warm towels after a nice cold swim
G o, go, go, back to our home

Stephanie Abe (8)
St Lewis Catholic Primary School, Croft

Best Holiday

The best day ever was when we went to the tent
There were meadows
The sand was shaped like hands
Waves washed the sand hands away
Creamy, greeny ice cream van
Rocks upon the shore
Now the town has changed
Zoom broom arcade games
A dark mark outside now sleeping
All I can hear is weeping
That was the best day ever.

Alice Walker (8)
St Lewis Catholic Primary School, Croft

Football

F ootballers sprinted across the pitch
O ut of the blue, one of the players scored a goal
O ur players were awesome last match
T he net was as big as a mountain
B alls were flying all across the pitch like birds
A footballer signed a man's shirt
L eading players they score again
L ifting the trophy the crowd chant.

Brenley Chadwick (9)
St Lewis Catholic Primary School, Croft

The Lost Girl

I can see her having fun
I can see her under her hair
I want to be her, having fun
I want to, I really hope
I go to the forest, that's my only friend
"I want to be pretty like her," I say to my friend, the river
I say to him
"I see my friends, they have been through a lot,"
I say, "But why can't I be like you?"

Annabelle (10)
St Lewis Catholic Primary School, Croft

I Am A Console

I am very fun to use
There's loads of controls and buttons
There's over a million games

I am very popular
Everybody loves me
I am red, black and blue
There are loads of different settings
The console is mostly made for Mario
The guy with the big moustache
And his best friend is Luigi

What am I?

Answer: A Nintendo Switch.

Joseph Lander (7)
St Lewis Catholic Primary School, Croft

Sadness

S ad is not fun and not nice
A ww it makes me teary when someone else is sad
D epression strikes again
N othing new, nothing else to do, for today just cry and cry
E ven silliness doesn't help or cure sadness
S ame thing every day, if you at least cry one tear it will ruin your whole day
S een everywhere, don't try it too. So you'll turn into a ruined life.

Jan Herman (8)
St Lewis Catholic Primary School, Croft

CR7 Poem

I play football
I used to wear a red shirt
I don't like Messi
I am the best
I am Mbappé's idol
I have never won the World Cup
My nickname is CR7
IShowSpeed is my biggest fan
I have won five Ballon d'Ors
My nationality is Portuguese
I have scored an amazing bicycle kick
I've played for Juventus, Real Madrid, Man Utd and Al-Nassr.
Who am I?

Answer: Cristiano Ronaldo.

Hugo Wells (7)
St Lewis Catholic Primary School, Croft

The Red Dragon

Cold sleepy dragon
Heavy rain from above
Fire coming from the dragon
Scary fox in the woods
The big bear ate a rabbit
I went camping and saw a dragon
The red dragon burned a city
The red dragon killed a dog
The red dragon destroyed a village
The dragon met another dragon
The dragon is really feisty
The red dragon changed colours
The dragon made a family
The red dragon is dead
The red dragon killed a monkey.

Tobias Mullin (10)
St Lewis Catholic Primary School, Croft

Nightmare

N ightmares have creepy wolves growling like a bear
I n your nightmare, snakes hiss like a broken tap
G reen ugly trolls moan and groan like a bored child
H orrible smells float like clouds
T ricky little gremlins squeak like mice
M ean old witches cackle like villains
A mazing dragons soar like bats
R ed blood seeps out of a zombie like water
E xcellent purple lanterns levitate like a hovercraft.

Aimen Jafar (9)
St Lewis Catholic Primary School, Croft

Snow Falls

A frosty night eating warm churros
Looking at the brightest light you have ever seen
Walking through sparkling snow with fluffy Uggs on
Watching the fireworks
You can see pretzels on the stove
Warm crepes melting in your mouth
Roasting marshmallows
Looking at the lights changing colours
You can see the trees blending into the dark
You can get a hot chocolate with marshmallows
Look up and there are beautiful shimmering stars
To finish off the night, one last snowball fight
Back home all cosy in bed!

Ruby Smith (9)
St Lewis Catholic Primary School, Croft

Out Of This World

The universe is big, a very big mystery,
It's a very important part of mankind's history,
Space goes on for more than infinity,
Saturn's ring is actually quite slippery!
Another planet, Mars,
Could probably fit inside a lot of cars,
Imagine going to space in a shiny red rocket. *Whoosh!*
Shrinking the moon to fit in your pocket.
Is anything more beautiful than a supermodel's face?
One of those many answers is space,
Our world is more than half polluted,
And you can be the one to stop it.

Ayrton Rushbrook (9)
St Lewis Catholic Primary School, Croft

Butterfly

B utter is sweet. So am I, but I have butter in my name because I like it.
U p, up and they're gone away, but not in the clouds though.
T ell me stories about this beautiful animal that flies in the sky.
T errific colours all around their bodies,
E ach shimmers all day all around.
R ight away they will fly away, up in the sky
F ly away, fly away, I am flying to you in the final distance
L ove me even though I'm up in the sky
Y ou're beautiful and I am too, with my colours.

What am I?
I'm a butterfly!

Harper Barnes (7)
St Lewis Catholic Primary School, Croft

Friendship Fairies

Fairies are...

F air as mean trolls
A mazing as rainbow unicorns
I maginable as the Tooth Fairy
R ed as an
I ncredible dragon
E legant yellow wings as bright as the
S un

A s pretty as pink sunflowers
R ed hair as red as a small apple
E xcellent as a little ant

T errific as pink sheep
H appy as a little puppy
E xcellent as a rainbow cat

B rilliant as colourful fireworks
E xcellent as rainbow hair
S illy as a crazy clown
T errific as a toy bear.

Alice Mould (7)
St Lewis Catholic Primary School, Croft

Avengers

A vengers assemble, Avengers assemble, it's always a bad day, but do not fear because the Avengers are here, they're going to save the day.
V ending machines that spew out evil deeds for the villains of Manhattan to plot their evil plans.
E nd of all the fights that gave me a fright, but now heroes are fighting which is more of a fright.
N ever ever fear, Avengers are here.
G reen Goblin is here and the Avengers are here to stop him.
E ndless attacks from villains, got to save Manhattan.
R ed suits, yellow suits, he's got them all, he'll shoot them and then they'll fall.
S uperheroes of Manhattan are Avengers!

Huw Barker (8)
St Lewis Catholic Primary School, Croft

Friends Forever

Harry Cypinter was at the park
With his friend Karl, when it was light,
They played all day until it was night,
Then a magical ball came down from above,
Then the two mothers cuddled like they were in love,
When they looked at the ball, it was shaped like a cone,
Then Harry's mother said, "Time to go home."
When they were about to go home, there were sad faces,
But Karl had magical laces,
Harry said, "Are we in a magical park?"
Karl said, "No, it's like we're in the boat of Noah's ark."
"Bye," said Harry,
"Bye," said Karl,
They will remain best friends,
Saying, "Bye forever and ever," until they die.

Thomas Warren (9)
St Lewis Catholic Primary School, Croft

Looked around and found the portal,
On the last day, I defeated the Ender dragon,
And even found the end ship and got an elytra.

Emma Wall (9)
St Lewis Catholic Primary School, Croft

Minecraft Survival

On day one, I got some wood from trees and made some materials,
And also, got stone tools,
At noon, I found a village and got some haybales for some bread,
And I also stole a bedroom, a house and looted all of the chests,
On the second day, I went into caves to find some ores and coal,
I even found five diamonds,
I made iron armour and tools,
I threw my iron pickaxe away and made a diamond one,
When it was day three, I made a Nether portal,
And got a golden helmet because otherwise, the piglins would chase me,
When I was in the nether,
I found a fortress and killed blazes to get blaze rods,
I also found a bastion,
So, I stole the gold and traded it with piglins to get eyes of Ender,
On the fourth day, I found the stronghold,

The Dutch lose out as England cruises through,
To go and play Spain in the last two,
This is where England's dreams finally come to an end,
As they lost to Spain, what a sad weekend.

E xciting tournament ahead
U npredictable who wins
R eady to kick off
O r watch Copa America.

Miciah Thornton (9)
St Lewis Catholic Primary School, Croft

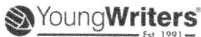

England's Euro Dream

In Germany the Euros were held this year
The citizens were all full of cheer
When the group stages have all been decided
They kick off the games
The Euros have started!

All 24 teams hope to get the trophy in their hands
First up Germany V Scotland
6-1 was the final score
Germany scored 6
And Scotland were poor

In England's group they faced Serbia, Slovenia and Denmark
They reached the top
Kicking the other teams out of the park
To the knockouts they go
Taking on the Slovakian team
Who wanted to ruin England's Euro dream.

England's dreams remain, Switzerland next in the quarter-final,
A difficult game in England's survival,
It goes to penalties and England win 5-3,
Off to play the Netherlands in the semis - yippee!

The World Of Fortnite

F ortnite is made by Epic Games
O ver the last few days there have been rare
R eload has been released
T o get better in Fornite, play training
N ew skins are added
I f you have no skins, buy V-Bucks
T otally, it's fine
E very update there are new things

B attle Pass you get free skins
A mazing, because you can get 100 V-Bucks
T ools like pixels
T o get levels just play XP Glitches
L oot up and pick up, you are loaded
E liminations give you an XP

P asses get you more skins
A lthough you get V-Bucks a lot
S cary skins for Halloween
S keleton ones.

Fortnite.

George Lander (9)
St Lewis Catholic Primary School, Croft

Animals

A dorable fluffy pets
N ever treat them badly
I guanas are interesting animals
M ice like to scurry for cheese
A ll animals are lovely and cute
L ions are big cat kings
S ave endangered animals.

Holly Ironside (10)
St Augustine Of Canterbury C of E VA Primary School, Belvedere

Summertime

Summer is here,
Winter is gone,
Flowers sprout high with colour,
As barbecues turn on.
As I say bye,
To the chilly breeze,
I say hello,
To the comforting warmth of the sun.
Snowy days are over,
The water fights come,
It's the sun's time to shine,
It is summertime.

Tisa Prajapati (10)
St Augustine Of Canterbury C of E VA Primary School, Belvedere

Fly, Little Bird, Fly

When there is snow
You need some place warm to go
So, fly little bird fly
Into the darkest of skies

Flying over harsh seas
Having no rest upon the trees

Life for you is very rough
But do try to be tough
I know you have to fight
For every single bite

Working ever so hard
With your courageous heart

When you reach your place
It truly makes you ace
Finally having a rest
Being the queen of your own nest.

Vivithra Arunagiri Babu Sailesh (10)
St Augustine Of Canterbury C of E VA Primary School, Belvedere

Snowflake Lace

Snowflakes fall, with
Delicate grace
Each one a piece of
Heaven's lace
Like covering the world
In a gentle embrace
On the soft white ground
Trees as white as can be
Winter's beauty in every space.

The winter beauty is the most delicate thing I've ever seen everywhere
It's full of white snow on the trees like wedding cake icing like never before
When summer comes it melts to the ground then after, Autumn the snow then returns.

Blessing Akeredolu (10)
St Augustine Of Canterbury C of E VA Primary School, Belvedere

Season Festival

Roses are red
Violets are blue
Flowers bloom in the spring
Because of the good luck it brings

In summer it's hot
To sweat, rapidly trot
We want summer to be cooler
But annually, it becomes crueller

Autumn; the season of crunchy leaves
One of the best seasons I believe
A colourful season
To convince me otherwise, give me a reason

Then there's the season of presents
When the holy spirit is in our presence
Hearts racing after Christmas and New Year's Eve
This is why people call it the best season and nobody wants it to leave

And if it leaves there is grief
But what is the best season?

Ethan G (10)
St Augustine Of Canterbury C of E VA Primary School, Belvedere

The New Girl In Town

There's a new girl that's moved to town, just a few doors down
That the whole school has been talking about.
Because, ever since she came
Everything around town has been strange.

Like when a boy asked her out
At the park they hung around.
They went to the shops and were heard laughing out loud
But since this day the boy was never found.

And last week at 6pm
I went out to see a friend.
And when I passed by her fence
I heard a bang coming from her shed.

So I climbed over the wall
Through the grass I had to crawl.
And when I opened up the shed
I found...

I say it now and I'll say it again
The girl next door, might not be your friend.

Zenzele Russell-Jess (10)
St Augustine Of Canterbury C of E VA Primary School, Belvedere

The Dinner Lady's Secret

The sun was shining on the beach
Shining with all its greatest might
Even though it wasn't an extraordinary spotting of light
It was good enough for everyone's summer sight
The only person who could give me some wisdom
Was the old dinner lady who faced racism

I asked the old lady, "Why is the sun orbited?"
She replied, "Good question, but I really don't know why."
I asked her another question, "Why do you look so down?"
She replied, "Look, sweetheart, I'll tell you a secret
But don't tell anyone, okay?"
So I made a promise with the dinner lady
So she said, "My husband died last week which is why I do not feel happy."

Temidayo Salako (10)
St Augustine Of Canterbury C of E VA Primary School, Belvedere

Autumn!

Harvest festival,
Comes around.
Bushes and fresh blackberries,
Can be found.

For some,
The school day has begun.
The summer holiday,
Has been and gone.

September, October,
Bring dark nights.
A cosy, warm coat.
To wrap up tight.

The insects now,
Seem far and few.
The trees grow bare,
A sky less blue.

First came blooming spring,
Then came the blazing hot
Summer sun,
Now the autumn
Has begun.

Navya Gohel (10)
Rushey Mead Primary School, Leicester

Mythical Lands

Inside the castle lies the princess
Old and young
Bright and smart
Unicorns guarding magical fences
Where dragons roam
The melody of birds are heard
Magical fairies are seen
Sweeping castle floors
Weeping the fresh-cut grass
Vegetables are pulled from the gardens of lush
Cooked into delicious meals
Where the smell floats around
No one comes to this magical world
Where all sorts of things happen
Fairies picking berries
Dragons sleeping on cushions
Princesses looking at flowing water.

Meghana Jivan (10)
Rushey Mead Primary School, Leicester

The Spine-Chilling Dream At Midnight

It's 12 o'clock at night
And I am full of fright.
Behind the shed,
Underneath my bed,
There are unnerving creatures.
Let me try taking pictures.
They speak as loud as 100 ringing bells.
Eww! Now something smells.
My door starts to creak,
As all the creatures start saying,
"There comes face freak."
Behind the shed,
There's a tall tree that indicates death,
So called the death tree.
Oh, I wish I could flee.
Just before I could scream,
I woke up and found out
That this was all a dream.

Prusti Parikh (10)
Rushey Mead Primary School, Leicester

Whispers Of The Wind

The wind hums softly through the trees
A melody that bends the breeze
It speaks in whispers, old and wise
Telling tales of distant skies

Each leaf it carries, light and free
Dances with a quiet glee
A story written, yet untold
In every gust, a secret gold

Beneath the sky, the earth stands still
But hearts are moved by time's own will
We wander through this fleeting day
Chasing dreams that drift away

It whispers words of distant lands
Of ancient seas and golden sands
It knows the paths we long to find
The dreams we've left, the hopes we bind.

Aarav Kuikel (10)
Rushey Mead Primary School, Leicester

Lost In The Galaxy

Stars shooting and gleaming,
Planets orbiting and spinning slow,
Confused about where I am,
Am I lost in a different universe,
Or lost on another planet?
Abnormal creatures hiding from me,
As if I am a harmful beast.
Awe-inspiring scenery played right in front,
Jaw dropped, I looked around.
It was so beautiful and magnificent,
I couldn't help but stare.
Everything was rare,
The sky super pretty,
Something I had never seen, my entire life.
The most beautiful cosmic object you can observe,
Is the one, the only,
Planetary nebula, that shows at the final stage of a star's life,
But my world seemed far.

Mahi Carsane (11)
Rushey Mead Primary School, Leicester

The Man's Journey

Beautiful butterflies that flap,
But there is a man needing a map.
He needs to find a way,
It is sunny so it might be May.
It is hard for him to go,
Shouldn't he show.
Being very brave,
Suddenly, he met a man called Rave.
They decided to work as a team,
Walking through the forest was a scream.
They went toward the noise,
But they didn't have a choice.
So they went to see,
On the way they saw a blue sea.
Then they went there,
Therefore we saw a parrot there.
They continued the journey,
Then Rave told a joke and it was funny.
Also they had the funnest journey ever,
They wouldn't stop, like, never.

Chreshta Deva (10)
Rushey Mead Primary School, Leicester

Diversity's Dream

Diverse dreams dance like dazzling stars,
Cultures converge, like multiple colours in jars,
Voices vibrate in vast visions of other people,
Together we all rise, a united steeple.

Like a garden, blooming, bright and bold,
Each unique petal, a story told.
Heartwarming heart, like sweet honey and hive,
In unity, we truly strive.

Asia's vast and ancient lands,
Africa's diverse, with golden sand.
North America's wide and free,
South America's lush with Amazon's spree.
Antarctica's icy, pure and bright,
Europe's history, a cultural light.
Oceania's islands, a paradise to see,
There's so much in the Earth's sea.

Khashni Ramdas (10)
Rushey Mead Primary School, Leicester

The Little Car (La Petite Auto)

The 31st of August 1914
I left Deauville a little before midnight in Rouvere's little car
With his driver, three of us
We said goodbye to a whole era
Furious giants stood over Europe
The Eagles were in a hurry to know each other thoroughly
The dead were trembling with fear in their dark dwellings
The dogs were barking at borderlines
I was carrying with me all the armies that were fighting
I felt them rising within me, spreading out, standing out
Snaking through the countries within the forests, happy villages of Belgium, Francorchamps and Eau Rouge
And the Pouhons Railway darting alive in colourful life
Deep oceans where monsters were stirring in the old carcasses of wrecks.

Mayank Salanki (11)
Rushey Mead Primary School, Leicester

Space Dragon VS Space Phoenix

As the space-bat-angel-dragon sings,
It notices four sets of wings,
Soon, realisation *dings*,
Then, it says, "That's my friend."

Up higher in the Milky Way,
There's a lane of fire and chain,
As big as seventy-seven lions' manes,
It's quite frankly World War Three.

The phoenix tries to flap its wings, but,
Ouch! The dragon eats one,
With totally no fatalities left,
It's left to cower in fear,

Or is it? With one last resort,
It eats the fire and takes all of its energy.
Suddenly, breathes it out!
After two days of fighting,
It's finally over.
"Truce?" called the phoenix.
"Truce," replied the dragon.
And they lived happily ever after.

Yug Mukesh (10)
Rushey Mead Primary School, Leicester

Dragon

In the shadowed realms where the wild winds weave
dwells a dragon fierce and proud, hard to believe
Scales, shimmering silver, glisten in the moonlight
Fiery breath, a torrent, ignites the velvet night
Claws, crafted from the darkest obsidian stone
Majestic wings spread wide, a tempest they invoke
A guardian of secrets amidst the ancient smoke
Eyes like molten gold, piercing through the gloom
With cunning intelligence, it spells impending doom
In tempestuous twilight, the titan takes flight
Fierce flames flicker, igniting the night
With scales like sapphire, shimmering and bold
A sovereign in the shadows
Fierce stories untold
Majestic, the monster, over mountains it soars
Breathing storms of power, its tempest roars
Glistening eyes gleam like gems in the gloom
Prophetic and potent, foretelling impending doom
In caverns of chaos, its cry reigns supreme
The fierce dragon dances in a nightmare's dream.

Kishan Patel (10)
Rushey Mead Primary School, Leicester

No hope remains, no chance to see
The Earth, so distant, a memory.
The traveller's journey, a tragic end,
Lost in the cosmos forever to transcend.

Nisarg Suman (10)
Rushey Mead Primary School, Leicester

Lost In Space

A cosmic voyage, a journey unknown,
Through star-strewn skies, a lone traveller's drone.
A spacecraft adrift, a ship without a crew,
Lost in the vastness, a universe new.

No guiding stars, no friendly beacon's light,
Just endless darkness, a chilling sight.
The ship's engine hums, a mournful sound,
As it aimlessly drifts, lost and unbound.

The captain's chair, a vacant throne,
Once a leader sat, now all alone.
The instruments flicker, a ghostly show,
As the ship wanders where no mortals go.

The stars, like diamonds, scattered and bright,
Yet offer no comfort in the endless night.
The planets, distant, cold and far,
A lonely traveller, a meandering star.

A message sent, a plea for aid,
But lost in the void, a desperate rage.
The ship drifts on, a silent tomb.
A cosmic gust lost in eternal doom,

Daydream

D on't run
A t night, who knows?
Y ou're next...
D own far
R ound the corner
E ast of the woods
A pproximately late
M idnight lurks again.

Chloe Horrocks (10)
Rice Lane Primary School, Liverpool

The Forest Of Humanity

F alling down all around
O n the forest of humanity
R efreshing air everywhere
E merald-green leaves swaying in the breeze
S limy snails leaving trails
T owering trees in the horizon.

Jathursa Uthayakaran (10) & Phoebe
Rice Lane Primary School, Liverpool

Summer Is Beautiful

Summer is the most beautiful season of the year.
Everyone is filled with smiles and happiness,
The skies are as blue as the ocean,
The trees are as green as broccoli,
The water is as clear as glass.
The shade is as cool as a cucumber.
The children's smiles are as bright as the sun,
Our minds blossom like beautiful daisies.

Lillie Macfarlane (9)
Rice Lane Primary School, Liverpool

Nature Is Strong!

Roses have thorns,
Deer have fawns,
Caves have gems,
Flowers have stems.

Rivers flow,
Trees grow,
Rain pours,
A lion roars.

The sky is blue,
Fish swim through,
Robins are red,
Cheetahs run ahead.

If you look to the right,
You can see the hillside,
Nature is strong,
But not for long.

Maya Sutton Nielsen (10)
Rice Lane Primary School, Liverpool

Magic Is All Around

Stars are magic
Everywhere's magic
Bluebells tiptoe around
Maybe they sound
Butterflies are dancing spirits
Rainbows are colourful pieces of hope
Ants keep their anger in and they cope
Daisies are full of life
Worms always have a wife
Robins are twirling owls
A bear is a tiger male
Bulls are fierce whales
Magic is all around.

Sophie MacDonald (10)
Rice Lane Primary School, Liverpool

My Favourite Bear Is A Panda

I love pandas, my favourite bear of all
Cuddly and soft as they laze along on the floor
The quietest bear in China
There are only just a few
Whose favourite thing to do all day
Is eat lots of bamboo!
Fearless and fluffy
They swim and they climb
I want one I can love and call mine!
Pandas are amazing
They really are, that's true
As well as eating bamboo
They enjoy doing kung fu!

Ellena Douglas (9)
Rice Lane Primary School, Liverpool

BFFs

Emily + Sophie = the best of friends,
Will always be together,
'Til the very end,
Laughing and playing, all day long,
Sitting there, right by the pond.
Emily and Sophie, having fun,
Emily and Sophie, eating lunch.
We're the best of friends,
So let's have fun,
We will be the ones to care,
When you're in despair,
So let's have fun,
With Emily and Soph

Thank you (drops mic).

Sophie Cunliffe (9) & Emily McDermott (8)
Rice Lane Primary School, Liverpool

Dream High, Fly High

Dream high,
Fly high,
Follow your passions, your dreams,
Fly like your passion.
Butterflies fly, so do you,
Don't give up your dreams,
Fly like butterflies.
Don't cry,
You're fine,
Safe hands are with you,
Now fly.
Fly like a butterfly,
Fly high like a butterfly,
Fly as high as a butterfly,
Never give up.
Feel like you're in Neverland.
Neverland?
Or call it,
Dreamland.

Cali Gray (10) & Lois Sheridan (9)
Rice Lane Primary School, Liverpool

Betty

B etty, my dog, sometimes runs away and we have to chase her to get her back into the house,
E xcitable is this little dog, she loves to say, "Hello" to everybody,
T his dog is my best friend, I always cuddle her and she always cuddles me,
T ickles and rubs on her belly are what she loves the most,
Y apper would be a great description for my Betty, especially when we go on walks and she says, "*Woof!*"

Martha Taylor (10)
Rice Lane Primary School, Liverpool

Cat's Glory

In the sunbeam's glow, a cat takes a nap,
In a soft, cosy lap.
With whiskers that twitch, and eyes gleaming bright,
She pounces on shadows, a true feline knight.
A flick of her tail, a playful little leap,
She chases the dreams that dance in her sleep.
With a purr and a stretch, she rules her domain,
In a world full of wonder, she will always reign.
In the quiet of twilight, the cat weaves through the shadows,
A whisper of mystery, cloaked in soft fur and moonlight.

Isaac Spence (10)
Rice Lane Primary School, Liverpool

Africa! Africa!

I am the son of the soil,
An indigene of Africa.
Africa my home,
Africa my dwelling place.
Africa my beginning, Africa my ending.
I am proud to be Africa,
They say I'm black;
I say I'm not black but brown.
Africa the place where Christ took refuge,
Christ took refuge,
Africa the home of gold,
Silver and diamond
Africa my birthplace
Africa the land of culture
Africa the land of my ancestors
Africa my beginning, Africa my
Ending.

Allan Mavuto (9)
Rice Lane Primary School, Liverpool

The Kingdom Of Nature

Emma was called Emma.
The girl loved nature.
Emma lived in a kingdom full of nature.
The girl's parents also loved nature.

Emma knows a lot about nature.
Emma knows all the different leaves and the different flowers and trees.
Emma loved her mum and dad.
Her mum and dad always bought her mini plants and seeds to plant herself.

Emma also lived with her grandparents.
Emma loved her grandparents.
Emma went to nature school.
Emma was ten years old.

Freya Gregory (9)
Rice Lane Primary School, Liverpool

Oh My Butterfly, Where Have You Gone?

Oh my butterfly where have you gone?
Where shall you be?
Under the tree?
Where shall you be?
Under the rocks?
I hope not.

Oh my butterfly where have you gone?
Where do you glide?
On the hill with the wonderful grass, nature and more.
Where shall you be?
Up in the tree?
Aah, I can't see.

Oh my butterfly how do you flutter your wings?
With glee and joy?
Oh there you are on my nose.
How could I not know?
Oh, you're light as a feather.

Olivia Toner (9)
Rice Lane Primary School, Liverpool

Stop Pollution!

In school, we learned about pollution
And we looked at some pictures of the sea.
On the pictures, we saw rubbish (pollution) in the sea.
Instantly, I thought, stop, stop pollution I say!
I was scared that everyone kept littering.
It is illegal to litter.
I was so shocked about everyone
Disrespecting our environment like that!
I was furious, raging with anger.
I didn't know what to do.
The sea creatures' lives are at risk.
So please, don't leave stuff on the ground
And please don't kill the environment.

Lucy Edwards (9)
Rice Lane Primary School, Liverpool

So I sneak into the room
I switch the lights on and off
Yes, it worked
But I never made it out
Until today.

Malachy Patrick (10)
Rice Lane Primary School, Liverpool

Wonder Palace

I am wonderstruck in this world
I look up at the Wonder Palace
As the rooms light up, the wonder starts
The toy soldiers march
And the flowers blossom
The sky is bright
And all is nice
Also, trees rise
But the light is off
Run! It's coming
Suddenly, the light is off
The sky is grey
Plants died
Trees died
Animals died
It's just me
Suddenly, the sky flickers
What is this?
A dream? No
Suddenly, it's back
All of it
But no, no
It is fake

Let's Be Heroes For Our Planet

The trees are green and blooming brightly
The seas are clean and marine life lives happily.
They say it will never change and will always stay this way
But only if we put our time and effort into keeping it this way.

But now things are changing and the world doesn't seem the same.
Seas full of plastic, pollution and wildlife dying
We can't go back, so let's step up and make a change.

So let's be heroes for our planet
We have to believe to achieve!
Recycle, reuse and revitalise
Make small changes to get rid of the dangers!

Sophie Mason (10)
Rice Lane Primary School, Liverpool

The Mighty Reds

I've got lots of favourite players,
Too many to name,
But I'll tell you about a few that play the beautiful game...
Virgil is our captain,
Our leader at the back,
And Jota is our striker,
Who leads the attack.
Lucho is our dribbler,
Who plays left wing,
And on the opposite side is our Egyptian king.
Dom, Ryan, and Macca are our midfield dream,
Then you've got Robbo and Trent,
The Scouser in our team.
We have Ibou and Alisson who protect our goal,
Then we have Arne Slot, who takes up the manager's role.
Last but not least,
We have the twelfth man,
Who stand on the Kop and sing as loud as they can.
I love football,
and Liverpool FC,
Come to Anfield on match days,
And that's where I'll be.

Sofia Tyrrell (11)
Rice Lane Primary School, Liverpool

I soon adapted to my schedule, embracing what I was given
Starting a new chapter in life.

Ava Fernandez (10)
Rice Lane Primary School, Liverpool

Starting A New Chapter In Life

I was happy where I was, but then I moved cities, which was hard
My family gave hugs and kisses the night before
Twisting and turning, thinking about the things yet to come
Then came the morning, leaving many memories behind
I knew where we were going, we'd make plenty more memories
Thinking about the journey made me think about my future
Will I make friends? Will I succeed in what I dream?
When I arrived, I was excited and nervous
I saw a small house with nice people in the neighbourhood
We unboxed our belongings one by one
Then we were ready to say home sweet home
A couple of weeks passed, then I was ready for school
New uniform, new environment to learn in
My teachers were nice as well as my class

All My Life

When I was a baby, all I'd do was sleep and eat
When I was a baby, all I'd do was enjoy getting pushed in my pram
When I was a baby, all I'd do was cry and order my mum to feed me

When I was a toddler, all I'd do was throw tantrums and hurt my mum
When I was a toddler, I got to see my little sister for the first time

When I was a child, I showed my first interest in football
When I was a child, I got to see my second sister for the first time
When I was a child, I joined my first football team

To this day, I still play football
To this day, I am still interested in football
To this day, I am the oldest sister
To this day, I am now in my last year of primary school
To this day, I am in the best place I could possibly be.

Lilah Fletcher (10)
Rice Lane Primary School, Liverpool

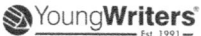

Hope

Hope is blue
Hope is like the ocean with no rubbish
Hope smells like freshly mown grass
Hope looks like no disease
Hope tastes like organic chicken drumsticks.

Amelia Leach (9)
Hanford School, Child Okeford

Joy

Joy is so yellow,
Jumping around a meadow.
Joy tastes like honey,
Or making lots of money.
It smells like red roses,
And looks like diamonds shining in the light.
Joy is happiness.

Lucia Xie (9)
Hanford School, Child Okeford

Happiness

Happiness is pink.
It tastes like sticky candyfloss
And smells like pretty roses
And looks like you are on a pink fluffy cloud.
It sounds like someone cheering
And it feels like a soft, pink blanket.

Georgie Bagley (9)
Hanford School, Child Okeford

Foal

Octopus legs
Bouncy thoughts
Frisky movements
Swooshing tail
Bounding strides
Occasional whines
Twisting ears
Silky mane
Precious eyes
Velvet nose
Munching mouth
Elegant neck
Dainty hooves.

Cordelia Plunkett (10)
Hanford School, Child Okeford

Winter

I see dead, forgotten leaves, gliding to the ground,
I smell warm, toasty, homely fires.
I hear the icy wind, swirling around my ears,
I feel winter's tight grip, tapping me on the shoulder.
I taste freshly cooked marshmallows, roasted over an open fire.

Beatrice Francis (10)
Hanford School, Child Okeford

Secrets

Secrets are a misty blue.
They taste like a dead fire, full of ashes and dust.
Secrets are the smell of a smouldering fire.
They look like a bat flying eerily through the air.
They are the sound of trees whispering and
The thought of someone grabbing me.

Bella Guinness (10)
Hanford School, Child Okeford

Secret

A secret looks like the sky full of clouds.
Exploding rain and making a horrible storm full of lightning.

A secret smells like fire burning the woods.

A secret sounds like popcorn
Popping out of its shiny shells.

A secret feels exciting
Like an adventure.

Lola Gonzalez (10)
Hanford School, Child Okeford

I Need A Poem

I need a poem,
But there is no time,
I want it to rhyme.
I lost my thought - it rhymed too -
Now I'm feeling so blue.
So I think and think,
And now I blink.
I had an idea,
But then I fled with fear -
What if my teacher said,
"Oh dear!"
How about a poem about not knowing?
Finally, I've found a poem!

Grace Strauss (10)
Hanford School, Child Okeford

A Poem About Nothing

I tried to think of a poem
I really, really did
But I just couldn't get any ideas
So I asked for help, I really did
But then I thought of an idea
One really quite unique
Why don't I say how I just could not think?

But then the idea went out of my head with a pop!
So I'm very sorry, but I don't have a poem
Full stop.

Allegra Aitken (9)
Hanford School, Child Okeford

This Is Me!

My imagination is like a wild party, but a hyena chased everyone away.
My imagination is a loud disco in my head.
My bedroom looks like a tornado has rushed right through and left a world of chaos behind.
My bedroom is a volcano about to erupt with gym kit, clothes, toys and books.
I am a fierce horse preparing to rear and bolt;
I am a balloon about to pop with craziness.

Beatrix Glendenning (9)
Hanford School, Child Okeford

Merry Christmas

C hristmas lights are amazing
H appy days for everyone
R oast potatoes boiling for Christmas!
I can't sleep - it's Christmas
S trange things happen at Christmas
T oys are sent from Father Christmas
M om is organising Christmas
A house full of people celebrating Christmas
S ay, "It's Christmas!"

Sofia Pardo (10)
Hanford School, Child Okeford

Silver Cat

The silver cat looks like the moonlight gleaming on the midnight sea.
The silver cat is a:
Leopard leaper,
Night creeper,
Rat killer.
It's glimmering, gleaming, shining like a shooting star,
But so quiet, so still, almost magical.
It draws you in like a siren,
It looks so soft, so calm,
But so energetic.
Soft, silky nose,
Smooth, fluffy fur,
Joyous spirit,
Quiet, creeping paws.

Moondancer!

Jemima Sellick (10)
Hanford School, Child Okeford

Christmas

C hristmas tree shining with baubles.
H anging sparkling trinkets.
R ed raspberry-like holly berries.
I nstant mouth-watering Christmas dinner.
S nood wrapped tightly around my crispy cold neck.
T oasted toes warming by the flaming fire.
M assive shining perfect presents.
A s beautiful as the Christmas star.
S hining ghost-white snow gripping my feet to the astonishingly cold ground.

Florrie Holland (10)
Hanford School, Child Okeford

What Is Gold?

What is gold? My dog was gold
As down the street, he strolled.
What is pink? My drink is pink
As it runs down the inky sink.
What is yellow? Strings are yellow
As they run down my cello.
What is blue? Blue penguins are blue
All sad locked up in a zoo.
What is white? A swan is white
Paddling in the silver lake at night.
What is purple? My turtle is purple
That I have named Myrtle.
What is grey? My cat is grey
As he stalks down the street on a rainy day.
What is green? Algae is green
As it flows down the stream.

Henrietta Heppenstall (10)
Hanford School, Child Okeford

I Am...

I don't know what to write,
But I'm having quite a fight
I want it to rhyme, but I don't have much time.
I will start here,
So come and hear.

I am red!
Roses growing up the garden shed.

I am orange!
Well, I'm simply just an orange.

I am yellow!
Calmly playing my cello.

I am green!
There's crashing lightning being seen.

I am blue!
A witch's bubbling stew.

I am purple!
The bumpy and smooth turtle.

I didn't know what to write
But I think I got it right.

Octavia Plunkett (9)
Hanford School, Child Okeford

My First Gallop

At first I thought I was going into a
Fast canter
But
Then I realised I was going into a
Gallop
And I gripped so tightly with my reins
And squeezed so tightly with my legs
I could feel the heartbeat of Tia
Then I looked down and I saw
The pounding of Tia's feet on the soft grass
I could feel the wind blowing on my face
I felt like I was flying
I could smell the mud being turned up
By the fast gallop of Tia's legs
At first, I thought I was going to fall off
But
Then I felt the rhythm of Tia's speed
I could feel my fear slowly moving away.

Eliza Robinson (10)
Hanford School, Child Okeford

Flock Of Sheep

F urry wool waving in the wind
L ochs of fluff flying away strand by strand
O n the hill dead wool wafting
C locks strike midnight - all the lambs are born (so the farmer thinks)
K icking and bleating, taking their first breath

O ff with the afterbirth
F ourth breath, still alive

S haking, shivering. Quick! Drink some milk!
H orses whining with delight
E ven though the farmer thinks the flock is done, there are still more lambs to come
E arth keeps going on
P eeing for the first time... fingers crossed it will stay alive!

Emily Fox-Pitt (10)
Hanford School, Child Okeford

Sadness Is Deep Blue

Sadness is deep blue.
It tastes like plain pasta.
Sadness smells damp and salty like a wet beach towel.
Sadness looks like puddles dotted around a quiet street on a cold winter's night.
Sadness sounds like a slow dripping tap and rain pattering against the windowpane.
Sadness tears me apart.

Excitement is neon pink.
It tastes like sweet and salty popcorn.
Excitement smells like churros mixed with chocolate.
Excitement looks like a thousand colourful leaves on a tree or a field full of fairground rides.
Excitement sounds like music on a carousel and kids giggling.
Excitement feels like staying up all night till Christmas day.
Excitement makes me fizz like lemonade!

Bea Mischi (10)
Hanford School, Child Okeford